Woodbourne Library
Washington-Centerville Public Library
Centerville, Ohio
DISCARDED

P9-CBI-917

why do
dogs
sniff
butts?

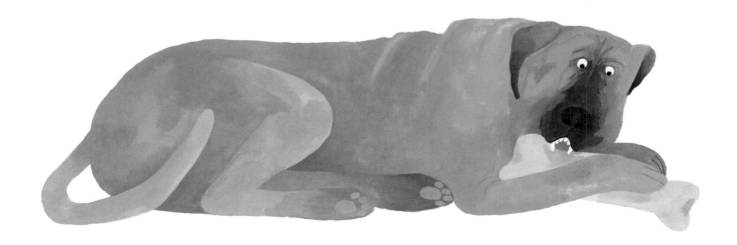

why do dogs sniff butts?

Curious questions about your favorite pet

Illustrated by Lily Snowden-Fine

Dog expert Dr. Nick Crumpton

 Thames & Hudson

Contents

Born to be tame

Are dogs still wild?

Once upon a time, dogs were wild animals that hunted and killed prey. Now they're the most popular pet in the world. This is all thanks to a friendship that began in the time of the hunter-gatherers.

Old friends

The earliest remains of a dog were found buried next to humans in Germany. Archaeologists think the remains are around 14,000 years old.

Wolf! Wolf!

A dog's closest-living relative is a wild animal: the gray wolf.

Canine housekeepers

Dogs have become more tame over the centuries. Humans have bred them to be useful for tasks like herding livestock, killing rats and mice, cleaning up campfires and guarding property.

Most popular pet

It became common to have a pet dog after World War II, when more people started living in cities. Dogs no longer had tasks, other than to be a good friend.

All dogs great and small

How many different dogs are there?

Dogs vary more in size, appearance and behavior than any other animal species. All together there are 339 different breeds, from the tiniest Chihuahua to the largest Great Dane.

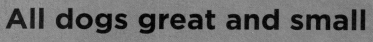

Tallest dog in the world
Freddy the Great Dane from Leigh-on-Sea in the UK is 41 in tall. He eats 2 lb of ground beef, 9 oz of steak and 10.5 oz of liver every day.

Smallest dog in the world
Miracle Milly is a Chihuahua from Florida in the U.S. who is only 3.8 in tall and weighs the same as 4 sticks of butter.

Dog with the longest ears
Harbor the Coonhound in Colorado in the U.S. uses his 13.5 in-long ears to pick up the smell of racoons by sweeping scents toward his nose.

Dog with the longest tail
Keon the Irish Wolfhound has a 2.5 ft-long tail and lives in Westerlo, Belgium.

Dog with the longest tongue
Mochi the St. Bernard from Sioux Falls in the U.S. has an incredibly floppy tongue at 7.3 in long.

9

Dog meet dog

Why do dogs sniff butts?

Dogs sniff each other's butts when they meet
to find out everything they need to know about
each other. It's like shaking hands with someone
and having a short conversation.

"Nice to smell you"
A dog's butt gives off chemicals
that tell other dogs all about them.
Sniffing another dog's butt is like
a human saying hello.

"Humans don't smell nothing"
A dog's nose has over 220
million smell sensors in it.
Human noses only have 5 million.

"You had chicken scraps for breakfast too?!"
The chemical messages given off by a dog's butt say whether the dog is male or female, whether they can have puppies, what kind of food they eat, and whether they're happy or sad.

"Message received, now don't distract me"
Just behind a dog's nose is the Jacobson's organ. This sends the messages attached to the smells of other dogs straight to the dog's brain. This is so other strong smells, like dog poop, don't distract the dog from receiving important information.

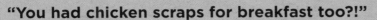

11

Get tails wagging

How do you speak dog?

Dogs see movement more clearly than they see color or pattern. By wagging their tails they can "speak" easily with other dogs. Here's how to decode what your dog might be saying:

Tail held at middle height:
"I'm relaxed"

Tail held straight up:
"I'm the boss"

Tail held horizontally:
"I'm listening"

Tail dropped:
"I'm anxious"

Tail tucked between legs:
"I'm scared"

Tiny, high-speed wag:
"I'm ready for action"

Fast wag:
"I'm excited"

Big wag:
"I'm pleased with myself"

Small wag:
"I'm here"

Fast wag to the right:
"I'm happy to see you"

Wag to the left:
"I'm not so sure about you"

Foreign accents

Dogs have all types of tails: straight, upright, curved, curled and corkscrew. This means they have different accents, or ways of talking, with their tails. If you're not sure what your dog is trying to say, check with a vet.

13

Herding dogs

Do dogs have jobs?

Herding dogs, or sheepdogs, have enormous amounts of energy and will chase anything that moves. Farmers find them useful for moving and controlling herds of sheep and cattle out in the open countryside. But this instinct can be a problem for cats who live with herding dogs!

Dog workaholics

Herding dogs are called working dogs in Australia and New Zealand because they have important jobs to do for farmers. On large farms where there are no boundary fences for hundreds of miles, Koolies and Australian Cattle Dogs help round up and count stock.

Hairy herders

Herding dogs are bred for working long hours in all weathers. Herders in hot countries have short hair and those in cold countries, like the Old English Sheepdog, have long hair.

Eye can see you
A Border Collie herds sheep by "giving them the eye," or glaring at them until they become scared, which is how wolves stalk their prey.

That'll do
Herding dogs learn commands very easily. "Steady" means to slow down, "Walk on" means to walk closer to the sheep and "That'll do" tells the dog they can stop working and come back.

Showtime

Why do dogs play dead?

Training dogs to perform tricks is the same as teaching dogs good behavior. Depending on the breed, dogs are motivated by what we offer them in return: praise, hugs, doggie treats or a comfy bed.

Hollywood star

One of the first canine film stars was a German Shepherd in the 1920s called Rin Tin Tin. He appeared in 27 Hollywood films over his career.

Do you feel lucky, punk?

Chinese Crested Powderpuff dogs may look like punks, but they're very eager to please. They learn tricks like turning on light switches and walking backward by being rewarded with cuddles and kind words.

Sporting show-off
Despite looking like a lamb, the Bedlington Terrier has a sporty body and competitive nature that sees it fly past the finish line in agility races.

Dead dog
Some wild animals freeze to protect themselves from prey. But dogs play dead as a way to win a tasty treat. Or to avoid a bath.

17

Mountain dogs

Why don't some dogs get cold?

For centuries, farmers in remote mountain locations have used dogs to protect their farm animals from wolves or bears. Over time, mountain guard dogs have developed ways to keep themselves warm, and their owners safe, in chilly climes.

Woolly parka
Bergamasco sheepdogs developed double, or corded coats to protect them from the cold, wet weather in northern Italy. The tough top coat of hair is twisted around the softer undercoat like a rope to create the effect of a waterproof parka.

Fat feet
All dogs' paws are made of fatty tissue to keep their feet warm on cold ground, but Newfoundlands also have webbed paws, like a duck. They help Canadian fishermen draw their nets in from the freezing cold water.

Doggy digs

The Malamute from Alaska can dig holes in the ground to create a shelter from snow and wind. A female Malamute will dig a large den for her litter of puppies.

Not so Zen

Lhasa Apso dogs have excellent hearing and can be very unfriendly towards strangers. They were bred to guard Buddhist monasteries in Tibet from the inside by alerting the monks to intruders as they entered.

Hunting dogs

Why are dogs good hunters?

Before dogs were domesticated they needed skills to help them to detect and capture prey to survive. Hunting prey was a wild dog's way of shopping for food. Domestic dogs still have these instincts and some can be trained to hunt different animals.

Hunt, point, retrieve
Golden Retrievers and Cocker Spaniels are trained to hunt game, point out its location and retrieve their catch with a "soft mouth." In other words, without sinking their teeth into it!

Follow that smell
Hungarian Vizslas naturally sniff out the scent trails of pheasants and pigeons, and are happy to run long distances to hunt them down.

Run, rabbit, run
Spanish Greyhounds were used for hunting hares and rabbits in open fields as long ago as 800 CE. Kings thought it was better to let their dogs do the work, saving them from getting their hands dirty.

Dog's best friend

Why are dogs so loyal?

Dogs and their wolf ancestors are pack animals, so forming devoted friendships with other animals is essential to their survival. In humans, dogs find protection and a source of food. Humans love dogs in return for being such loyal companions.

HACHICŌ

Loyal or peckish?

Every day, a Japanese Akita called Hachikō saw his owner off to work at a train station in Tokyo and waited until he came home. After his owner died, Hachikō continued to wait at the station for the next nine years. It's possible Hachikō was being loyal, but maybe he was being faithful to his stomach—the train station is surrounded by food stalls!

GOBI

Epic follower
Gobi, a stray dog, followed marathon runner Dion Leonard for nearly 80 mi during a race through the Gobi Desert. The pair grew so close that after the race, Dion named her Gobi and took the dog back to Edinburgh to live with him.

SUSAN

Royally loyal
Corgis have been loyal to the British royal family for decades. In 1944, when the Queen of England was still Princess Elizabeth, she was given a Corgi called Susan for her birthday. Susan is the ancestor of more than 30 of the Queen's Corgis since then.

Loud dogs

Why do dogs howl at sirens?

Dogs don't truly howl, but they do make howl-like calls to connect with their owners or other dogs. Their wolf ancestors used howling to locate one another in a canine version of texting. It is natural for a dog to howl back in reply to the sound of a siren because it is howl-like.

What's the difference between a bark and a howl?

Dogs usually bark at things or people, whereas a howl is intended to connect a dog with their pack. A Norwegian Elkhound will bark at a moose to move it towards a hunter, but howl to reach out to other dogs.

Howl are you?

Siberian Huskies are known for mimicking the sounds of people's voices, like YouTube sensation Mishka, who howls "I wuv you" for the camera.

I know that song!
Chelsea Greyhounds make a "rooing" sound that other Greyhounds can't help but sing along to.

Squeak along with me
Tiny, fluffy Pomeranians have a high-pitched howl that they make in response to other dogs.

A dog's scream is worse than its bite
Shiba Inus make an unusual screaming sound when they are interested in something.

Daily Tail

Dog heroes

Can dogs save lives?

Throughout the ages, dogs have been there to help, rescue and comfort humans in need. German Shepherds can be trained to obey a police officer without question. Beagles use their strong sense of smell to detect bombs. Labrador guide dogs help people who are blind or sight-impaired to avoid obstacles.

Rescued in the lick of time

Barry the St. Bernard rescued a young boy lost in an avalanche in the Swiss Alps, saving his life by licking the boy to warm him up.

Grace under fire

In the 1700s, Dalmatians were trained to run alongside horse-drawn fire carriages. While the firefighters battled the blaze, the dog stayed with the horses to keep them calm and to guard the carriage.

26

Canine war hero
Chips received both Silver Star and Purple Heart medals for helping soldiers in World War II. He dragged a phone cable across a battlefield so his platoon could call for help.

A listening ear
Lexy the German Shepherd works as a therapy dog in the military at Fort Bragg in the U.S. She helps psychiatrist Major Christine Rumayor treat soldiers suffering from trauma by making them feel calm when talking about difficult experiences.

Terriers and Dachshunds
Why do dogs dig?

Short-legged Terriers and Dachshunds have an natural desire to explore tunnels and dark holes. They are known for their pluck and were bred to hunt pests that burrow underground.

Nailed it!
A West Highland White Terrier's favorite pastime is digging. Their nails grow faster than most dogs, so they can dig better.

Adrenaline junkies
Teckels are wire-haired Dachshunds from Germany with higher adrenaline levels than most dogs. They are sized according to the type of holes they can fit down: rabbit (small), fox (medium) and badger (large).

Nose to the ground

Yorkshire Terriers have their noses closer to the ground than other dogs, so they can pick up scents more quickly. They were bred in the 1800s for catching rats in cotton mills in England.

Feisty gentlemen

Bull Terriers were cross-bred to have the qualities of a gentleman soldier: they would never start a fight, but would be able to finish one. They are also the only dogs with triangular eyes.

Gnarly dawgs

Why do dogs like surfing?

Some of the coolest dogs around are pro surfers and skaters. Dogs don't have the same sense of balance as humans do, but it seems many dogs get the same thrill when they feel the wind in their ears.

Hang loose
Ricochet the Golden Retriever started surfing when she was 8 weeks old and is now a pro dog surfer who hangs loose with disabled surfers.

Surf safety
Dogs have a lot of hair that makes them colder and heavier when wet. Although dog wetsuits don't exist, you can give your dog a little lifejacket.

Hang ten

Dogs can't grip with their toes like people can, but that doesn't mean they can't master classic surfing moves. In Hawaii, Night Hawk the terrier mastered the hang ten, letting eight of his toes hang off the nose of his owner's surfboard.

Beach bum

Not all dogs can swim, but many can skate. Tillman the English Bulldog became a champion skateboarder in California. He learned to push himself off to get rolling and tilt his body to steer.

31

Always hounding

Why do dogs chase cats?

Hound dogs will chase anything fast-moving that catches their eye, including rabbits and the family cat. With long, slender bodies and eyes that point forwards, rather than to the side, their bodies are built for high-speed chases.

Quite quiet

Whippets and Greyhounds seem like bold racing dogs, but they're actually very shy. Hero the Whippet's quiet nature makes her the perfect reading assistant for children learning to read in London.

Goldie locks

Afghan Hounds have a long, silky coat that looks like human hair. Some owners tuck their hound's ears into socks to keep them clean when eating.

Legging it
Ibizan Hounds love to sprint at high speeds, but they can be hard to stop once they've started.

Couch potato
Basset Hounds may have bursts of intense energy, but they spend the rest of their time curled up sleeping.

Media mutts

Why does my dog have more followers than me?

Dogs can be very entertaining, and their expressions and behavior are adorable to many. Before social media, a dog had to be owned by a well-known artist, movie star or reality TV star to become famous. Now every dog and its owner can build a fan base.

Mutt muses

Three very famous artists chose Dachshunds for companions and painted them into their pictures: Andy Warhol, Pablo Picasso and David Hockney. Mexican artist Frida Kahlo had lots of pets, including a few hairless Xoloitzcuintlis.

Funny face

Audrey Hepburn loved her Yorkshire Terrier Mr. Famous so much that she took him with her to movie sets. He appeared in a scene with her in the film *Funny Face*.

Sad face

French Bulldogs are now the UK's most popular dog after celebrities including Lady Gaga, the Beckhams and Hugh Jackman made them trendy. Their flat faces can lead to breathing problems and sadly, not all owners can afford to care for them.

Dogs online

Boo the Pomeranian was the world's first dog to have a social media account. Owned by Facebook employee Irene Ahn, Boo's Facebook page had over 16 million likes.

Home alone

What does my dog do when I'm gone?

Dogs are social creatures and can easily get lonely when they're left at home by themselves. They can start chewing the furniture, bark constantly, pace, ruin the carpet and get up to all sorts of mischief.

Not guilty

Scientists at the University of Cambridge in the UK have found that a dog can't feel guilt. The sorry face a dog puts on is simply the way it responds when its owner seems angry or disappointed.

Caught on camera

Pet parents of a Great Dane set up a spy camera at home and discovered that their darling dog was doing endless cannonballs in the swimming pool while they were at work.

Dogchat

New technology allows owners to communicate with their dog while they're away. Dogs can send doggie selfies and bark mail messages, which their owners can reply to with paw-activated treats.

Pawsome service

A new kind of social network connects dog owners in need of a dog walker with volunteers who love dogs but don't have one of their own.

Give a dog a bone

Why do dogs chew bones?

Chewing raw bones is a dog's way of brushing its teeth. It removes tartar, which causes tooth decay, and helps remove bits of food stuck in a dog's teeth. Raw bones can also be good sources of minerals and help a dog's digestion.

Feed your dog meat twice a day at regular times. Some dogs eat as much as they can every time they see food and have to be trained to stop eating when they are full.

Avoid feeding your dog chocolate and avocado, which can be toxic to dogs.

Make sure your dog has plenty of fresh water.

Like wolves, a dog has big canine teeth for ripping meat and strong molars for crunching bone. Never give your dog chicken bones though as they splinter too easily.

Potty training

Why does dog poop smell so bad?

Dog poop can spread diseases like toxocariasis which can lead to blindness in humans. It is important to pick up your dog's poop with a bag and put it in a trash can.

Message in the poop

A dog likes smelling another dog's poop because it communicates lots of information about who left it and how healthy they are.

Pooper scooper
The U.S's 89.7 million dogs produce 11,000 tons of dog poop every day. That's a lot of pooper scooping!

What a smell!
Dog poop smells so much worse to us than our own poop because humans naturally avoid the smell of things that are dangerous to us.

Mythical mutts

Who is the most legendary dog?

For thousands of years people have created legendary stories about dogs, often inspired by a dog's speed, strength or ferocity. In some cultures and religions dogs have even been worshipped as gods.

Grisly gatekeeper
In Greek mythology, Cerberus the three-headed dog watches the gates of Hades, where souls are sent to be tormented.

Ghostly guard dogs
In Welsh mythology the otherworld, Annwn, is guarded by ghost hounds called Cŵn Annwn.

Canine constellation

Canis Major is a group of stars in the night sky in the shape of a dog. In Greek mythology it is said to show Laelaps, the fastest dog in the world, who was destined to catch anything she chased.

Dog deity

The ancient Egyptian god Anubis had a canine head and a man's body. He watched over the dead and helped mummify Osiris, god of the afterlife.

Dog words

Adrenaline – a molecule found inside the body that, when released, increases an animal's heart rate and prepares it either for "fight" or "flight."

Archaeologists – scientists and historians who study the ancient remains of humans and their cultures.

Domestication – when humans change wild animals' behavior so that they become tame. This usually takes many generations of training and selecting the friendliest pups to breed.

Hunter-gatherers – humans who tracked and hunted animals to survive rather than raising animals and growing crops on farms.

Minerals – chemicals (like iron and zinc) that animals absorb from the food they eat, which helps them grow.

Predator – an animal that hunts other animals for food.

Prey – an animal hunted or caught by another animal for food.

Social – enjoying interacting with other dogs or humans, for instance being playful and friendly.

Species – a group of animals that look and act like each other. Dogs and cats are different species, as are humans and chimpanzees.

Tame – an animal that is comfortable or relaxed in the presence of humans.

Tartar – a hard, yellow layer of bacteria on teeth that, if not removed, can cause gum disease in an animal's mouth.

Toxocariasis – a disease caused by roundworms, parasites that live in dogs' digestive systems (and their poop), that can cause rashes, stomach pains, headaches and blindness.

Index

Why Do Dogs Sniff Butts? © 2020 Thames & Hudson Ltd, London
llustrations © 2020 Lily Snowden-Fine

All Rights Reserved. No part of this publication may be reproduced or
transmitted in any form or by any means, electronic or mechanical, including
photocopy, recording or any other information storage and retrieval system,
without prior permission in writing from the publisher.

First published in 2020 in the United States of America by Thames & Hudson
Inc., 500 Fifth Avenue, New York, New York 10110

www.thamesandhudsonusa.com

Library of Congress Catalog Card Number: 2019940730

ISBN 978-0-500-65223-7

Printed and bound in China by Shanghai Offset Printing Products Limited